MOUNTAIN SICKNESS
Prevention, Recognition & Treatment

D1010286

AMERICAN ALPINE CLUB
CLIMBER'S GUIDE

MOUNTAIN SICKNESS

Prevention, Recognition & Treatment

PETER H. HACKETT, M.D.

THE AMERICAN ALPINE CLUB
NEW YORK

Fourth Printing 1987

ISBN 0 930410 10 6

Printed and bound in the United States of America

Published by
THE AMERICAN ALPINE CLUB, INC.
113 EAST 90TH STREET
NEW YORK, NEW YORK 10028

Acknowledgements

Grateful acknowledgement is made to
Charles S. Houston, M. D.
and
I. Drummond Rennie, M. D.
for their critical review and helpful suggestions.

Contents

Introduction

THE past decade has witnessed an explosion in mountain traveling by skiers, backpackers, climbers, runners, hunters, fishermen and assorted mystics. There is now good wilderness medical information available, especially on frostbite, hypothermia and general first aid. This book is designed to fill the existing gap in specific and detailed information on acute mountain sickness. It is meant for both laymen and physicians and deals more with the practical aspects of concern to mountain visitors rather than the latest scientific advances in pathophysiology, although such references are included.

A number of authorities are quoted, though the

views expressed are those of the author. As Director of Medical Research and Medical Director of the Himalayan Rescue Association, I have had the opportunity to observe thousands of mountain hikers on the trail to Mount Everest in the village of Pheriche (altitude 4,243 meters or 14,000 feet) in the northeast region of Nepal. These trekkers have provided the experience on which this book is based. Obviously, then, it reflects my special experiences in Nepal.

Acute mountain sickness undoubtedly varies in incidence and onset, and perhaps somewhat in symptoms, in different parts of the world. Differences in mode of ascent (i.e. flying, driving or climbing to altitude), rate of ascent, level of exertion once on foot, absolute altitude reached, cold exposure, risk of dehydration, etc., will all interplay in the development of acute mountain sickness. With this in mind, this book attempts to generalize sufficiently to cover most high altitude situations, but obviously will not apply to all.

The spectrum of illnesses (or maladaptations) observed at high altitude include acute mountain sickness (AMS), high altitude pulmonary edema (H.A.P.E.), and high altitude cerebral edema (H.A.C.E. or just C.E.). The three categories overlap considerably, and dividing lines are necessarily arbitrary. Admittedly, this creates a bit of confusion which reflects our still relatively poor understanding of the problem. There are other altitude related problems such as retinal hemorrhages (bleeding spots in the back of the eye seen only with an opthalmoscope) which do not fall conveniently into any category. For the purposes of this discussion, acute mountain sickness is divided into three categories: mild, moderate and severe. Pulmonary and cerebral edema are included in the severe category of acute mountain sickness.

MOUNTAIN SICKNESS
Prevention, Recognition & Treatment

What is
Acute Mountain
1   Sickness?

ACUTE mountain sickness is a symptom-complex; that is, a *group* of symptoms usually appearing together, with variations among individuals. It is seen in people who have recently arrived at high altitude or have just gained altitude, and may start anytime from a few hours to a few days after ascending. *High altitude* is arbitrarily defined as altitudes greater than 3,000 meters (10,000 feet). People with heart and lung diseases may have difficulty at lower altitudes and, rarely, a healthy person will develop some form of acute mountain sickness as low as 2,500 meters (8,200 feet). Most commonly acute mountain sickness is seen above 3,000 meters (10,000 feet).

HEADACHE
INSOMNIA
LASSITUDE
LOSS OF COORDINATION (ATAXIA)
EDEMA OF THE EYES AND FACE

COUGH
SHORTNESS OF BREATH
FULLNESS OR TIGHTNESS
  IN CHEST
IRREGULAR BREATHING,
  ESPECIALLY AT NIGHT

LOSS OF APPETITE
NAUSEA
VOMITING

REDUCED URINE OUTPUT

WEAKNESS

LEGS FEEL "HEAVY"

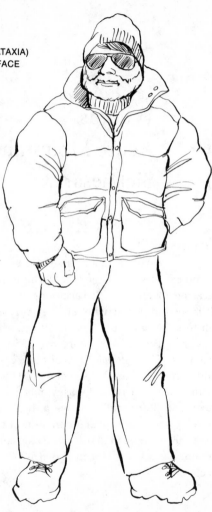

The symptom-complex is now well recognized, and the illustration shows the most common symptoms.

WHO IS SUSCEPTIBLE?

Anyone proceeding to high altitude is at risk of developing acute mountain sickness. *Some* individuals are inherently more susceptible, for reasons that are not understood. Others are rather resistant. Then again, susceptibility will vary in the same person from time to time. The tremendous individual variation is one of the more puzzling aspects of the illness. In those susceptible, ascending quickly will increase the likelihood of developing acute mountain sickness. Even the more resistant individuals may succumb if ascending fast enough. Those who have had acute mountain sickness in the past are likely to get it again if rate of ascent is the same. Younger persons are more at risk than older ones, only *partly* because they generally go faster. Studies at Pheriche have shown the incidence in men and women is the same. Physical conditioning has absolutely no influence on susceptibility. In fact, fit individuals tend to ascend faster and therefore may have a higher incidence.

Overexertion seems to contribute to acute mountain sickness, and dehydration may be a predisposing factor. (See Prevention.)

Recognition and Treatment of Symptoms

2

IT is important to differentiate acute mountain sickness, a sometimes fatal but easily treatable condition, from other problems that may present similarly. The presentation and significance of the common symptoms are discussed in detail, with suggestions for symptomatic treatment.

HEADACHE

Headache is by far the most common single symptom. In a recent series of 200 trekkers studied at Pheriche (Hackett and Rennie, 1978), 65 percent reported headaches. It can vary from a minor nuisance to a severe, incapacitating problem. The severity of the headache is a good guide to its significance. A mild headache which comes on after a hard day of hiking may well be due to exertion or sun, or heat or cold, rather than altitude per se. This will usually disappear with a rest, a cup of tea or coffee, or maybe aspirin or acetaminophen. It invariably disappears with a night's sleep and this type of headache is of little concern. The morning, on awakening, is a good time to judge symptoms from a viewpoint of acute mountain sickness. A headache that develops during the night and is present on waking is probably due to altitude, and should be taken more seriously. It will sometimes disappear just by deep breathing exercises or getting up and moving about—if so, it is of less concern. The real bell-ringing warning sign is a headache, usually moderate to severe, that persists despite aspirin or acetaminophen and perhaps 30 mg. codeine, and despite a night's rest. If there are no other symptoms of acute mountain sickness, and the person continues to ascend, there will usually be other symptoms shortly. A severe headache in itself may cause nausea and even vomiting. Such a headache, even if the solitary symptom, should be an indication to stop ascending and to descend if it is still present after a second night at the same altitude. Many climbers notice a headache on their *descent* from bination with headache, insomnia, or other symptoms, it helps establish the diagnosis of acute mountain sickness. Rarely does a person with acute mountain sickness have a good appetite, and the better the appetite at high altitude, the better that person is acclimatizing (assuming a fairly appetizing diet). Prolonged anorexia can lead to a state of weakness and poor nutrition which is aggravated by strenuous exercise. Nausea is quite common and usually subsides as mild acute mountain sickness passes and the person becomes better acclimatized. Vomiting is a more serious sign. If it is not accompanied by headache or other symptoms of acute mountain sickness, other causes such as "stomach flu" must be considered. If in combination with diarrhea, and perhaps fever and chills, it is usually gastroenteritis or dysentery, not acute mountain sickness.

Persons with nausea will become dehydrated if they cannot drink fluids. Those with frequent vomiting will suffer dehydration and lose precious electrolyte salts, especially potassium. Such persons should be evacuated to lower altitude before they become litter cases. Medication to control nausea and vomiting in acute mountain sickness usually has to be given rectally or by injection. Compazine or Phenergan suppositories or injectable solutions can be given. (See Appendix.)

Those going to higher altitudes will often experience symptoms of malabsorption. Digestion has been shown to be impaired, probably due to oxygen lack. The result is abdominal cramps and large amounts of gas after eating. In the third world, this condition has to be differentiated from common parasitic diseases such as giardiasis. Some doctors recommend high altitude climbers have digestive enzyme preparations at base camp. Although there are no studies to confirm this, I have found them quite helpful in reducing gas and abdominal cramps. They can be taken in tablet form (uncoated is best) a half-hour after eating.

PULMONARY SYMPTOMS

Cough may be dry or wet. The cold, dry air of the mountains in itself may be irritating and cause a deep, hacking cough, especially on exertion. The mucous membranes of the throat become very dry and cause an irritating, tickling sensation that makes one cough. Hard candies or throat lozenges (which comprise a large part of expedition medical kits) and adequate hydration (drinking *lots* of fluids) will usually help. Inhaling steam helps moisturize the throat and respiratory passages and is sometimes the only effective therapy. A frequent cough in association with severe breathlessness on exertion or even mild breathlessness at rest (when compared to one's companions) should alert one to the possibility of high altitude pulmonary edema (H.A.P.E.). Only in the advanced stages of H.A.P.E. will the cough start to produce pinkish or rusty-colored frothy sputum—until that point the cough may be dry. (See H.A.P.E.) A person whose cough is due to early pulmonary edema will also become weaker and have less endurance, whereas a cough due to environmental conditions should not affect strength.

A feeling of "fullness" in the chest is described by persons with congested lungs, i.e. early pulmonary edema. Actual chest pain is uncommon in H.A.P.E. and more common in a chest infection such as pneumonia or pleurisy, or with a cracked rib or torn cartilage, as often happens in severe coughing spasms. If pressing on the chest wall (ribs) causes the pain or aggravates it, it is more likely a musculo skeletal or infectious problem rather than H.A.P.E.

PERIODIC BREATHING

Irregular breathing is a common complaint at altitudes above 3,000 meters. It is almost always noticed at night, often by the person's tentmate or campmate. It is characterized by what is called "periodic breathing." Typically, there are four breaths or so, and then no breathing at all for as long as ten or fifteen seconds. The pattern then repeats, and can go on for hours at a time. The longer the period of no breathing (apnea) the more likely it is the person will awaken, usually to panic because he notices immediately that he is not breathing! Or, as has happened to many a camper, the tentmate will panic when he or she notices the apnea and will awaken their companion and encourage them to breathe. Trip leaders or doctors should explain this phenomenon to all the persons in a group going to altitude, to allay the panic reaction. Periodic breathing in the absence of obvious symptoms of acute mountain sickness seems to be quite harmless, and not a cause for worry. It is caused by a change in the control of breathing within the brain. The exact significance of this phenomenon is being investigated. Studies have shown that it is improved by acetazolamide (see Diamox) but we don't know if it *is* important to improve it. Periodic breathing may be significantly exaggerated in someone with high altitude pulmonary edema, but then there will be other symptoms as well.

LASSITUDE

Defined by Oxford's as weariness, indifference, fatigue. It is often difficult to differentiate from exhaustion, but most easily done by its time course. Exhaustion will respond to a day or night of rest, fluids, food, etc. Lassitude of altitude typically progresses over 24 to 48 hours and indeed, may be the only symptom initially. When the seemingly exhausted person, however, gets to the point where he cannot get up for meals, will not talk to anyone, and refuses to drink sufficient fluids, he soon cannot take care of himself and may rapidly progress into unconsciousness over the next 12 to 24 hours. This whole sequence may take place without a headache, no vomiting, and no noticeable shortness of breath. However, such a person will usually exhibit loss of coordination (ataxia) if carefully tested for it. Thus lassitude is a crucial sign to recognize, and if severe or associated with ataxia, it is an indication for immediate descent and oxygen if available. (See Cerebral Edema.) The entity to differentiate from acute mountain sickness when presented with these symptoms, in addition to exhaustion, is hypothermia.

ATAXIA (Loss of Coordination)

Another cardinal sign to watch for is ataxia. The cerebellum is the part of the brain controlling coordination of our various muscle groups, balance and spatial orientation. It is also a part of the brain with a very fast utilization of oxygen. Therefore it is quite sensitive to hypoxia, or oxygen lack. It is also impaired in cerebral edema. A dysfunction of this brain center, as evidenced by ataxia, is usually a serious sign. Fortunately, it is extremely easy to test for. Every single person with even the slightest degree of acute mountain sickness should be tested for the presence of ataxia. The easiest method of detection is the heel to toe walking test, also called tandem walking. This can be done in almost any situation as long as the person 1) is sober, and 2) has enough strength to stand up and walk. Police use it as a sobriety test (in the movies) frequently.

To do the test, draw a straight line in the snow, use an imaginary line, or point in a direction, whatever is most practicable. Then have the person start walking very slowly by placing the heel of the front foot against the toe of the back foot, and progress by taking short, one-foot steps, always placing heel to toe. This is best done without awkward boots and crampons and is obviously impossible with skis or snowshoes. Normally a person can perform the task without the balance maneuvers of a tightrope walker. Persons with mild ataxia will sway considerably and have some difficulty maintaining balance, but can walk this way ten or twelve feet without falling. Moderately ataxic individuals will step off the line and perhaps stagger. Grossly ataxic subjects will fall to the ground. Any degree of ataxia should be taken seriously. In a doubtful case, and perhaps best to do in most cases, use an apparently normal (and sober) companion (or oneself if necessary) for a comparison. Everyone in a cold, tired party may show mild ataxia. This is probably due to exhaustion, unless all are developing severe mountain sickness. Ataxia may also be seen in hypothermia.

The second test for ataxia is the Romberg. Have the person stand up straight, feet close together (touching) and arms at the sides (as if "at attention"). Face the subject and place your arms around his or her upper body, but not touching, and tell him you won't let him fall. Then have him close his eyes. Normal—there is very little movement, the person stands still. Abnormal—the person starts to sway and may even fall against your arms. One needs to wait only ten to 15 seconds for the maximal response. Again, comparison with a well companion is helpful. Sobriety is again essential. Marijuana in usual doses should not affect these tests.

All high altitude climbers, backpackers, wilderness travelers, etc., should be familiar with at least one of these simple tests. If you have the impression that someone in your party is developing serious mountain sickness, do a simple test for ataxia (or two). The abnormalities are usually so obvious and so impressive when compared to normals that no one in the party will doubt your judgment.

A study we recently completed, but have not yet published, showed that individuals with ataxia had dangerously low blood oxygen levels. This indicated to us that the ataxia may have been caused by the hypoxia (low blood oxygen) and not *necessarily* by cerebral edema, as was previously thought. It still seems best, however, to treat these people as if they had cerebral edema. Oxygen and descent are thus indicated. (See Cerebral Edema.)

A person with ataxia should never be sent down alone or with another sick member. Nor should he be left behind while the others go on, with the idea of retrieving him the next day or in the next few hours. He should be taken down immediately, with oxygen if available, and a descent of 300 to 1,000 meters may be necessary for recovery. Full recovery may take days or weeks. Once ataxia is present the "patient" can become a litter case in as quickly as six to twelve hours, and usually in 24 hours, if not treated appropriately. If there are no other signs or symptoms of acute mountain sickness, and the setting is appropriate for hypothermia or exhaustion, then it may be safe to stay at the same altitude and treat for these conditions. If, after warming and rest the ataxia persists, then descent is essential, with or without oxygen.

REDUCED URINE OUTPUT

This may be an ominous sign at altitude. It is difficult to evaluate, however, since dehydration alone produces the same thing and nearly everyone at altitude gets somewhat dehydrated. Regardless of the mechanism, a reduced (or even normal for sea level) urine output is *abnormal* at high altitude and should alert one to be wary of acute mountain sickness. Mild symptoms should be taken more seriously in the presence of reduced urine. To maintain a clear and copious urine output may mean, depending on conditions, intake of one to five liters (quarts) of fluids per day, or even more. (See Fluid Balance at Altitude.)

3   Peripheral Edema

PERIPHERAL edema is a common problem
at altitude and often quite dramatic. This refers to
swelling around the eyes and face, the hands, or the
ankles and feet, and is sometimes present in more
than one area. There is no associated pain such as in
swelling after an injury. It is caused by abnormal
fluid distribution and/or fluid retention. In a series of
200 trekkers whom Dr. Rennie and I studied, a full
23 percent had at least one area of peripheral edema,
and it was more common in women. It is most commonly seen in the hands, but this is the least likely
to be associated with acute mountain sickness. Rucksack strap compression, the swinging movement of

the arms, the cold and the sun may all contribute to hand swelling. The greatest danger is loss of blood supply to the fingers because of constriction from rings. At the first sign of edema, all rings should be removed.

Edema about the eyes and cheeks is more commonly associated with acute mountain sickness (14 out of 19 with facial edema in our study had acute mountain sickness). The eyelids can become so swollen that vision is impaired. It is worse on rising, for apparently the fluid accumulates during the night. During the day, when one is in the upright position, usually walking, the edema subsides somewhat. The next morning it can be worse, especially if more altitude has been gained, and then it may involve the entire face.

We have only rarely observed edema of the ankles and feet due to altitude. In the few cases observed, it was associated with other areas of edema as well, and with acute mountain sickness. Others have found a case of leg edema in a healthy person exercising in cold weather at *low* altitude.

Some experts feel that women are more likely to experience peripheral edema (and perhaps acute mountain sickness) just before their menses, since fluid retention at this time of the menstrual cycle is a common problem at sea level. We have not been able to show this to be true at altitude, but further studies must be done for a definite answer. Women who take mild diuretics (water pills) routinely for such fluid retention should do so at altitude as well, and perhaps more liberally.

One series of ten trekkers with peripheral edema was described in the Lancet (Hackett and Rennie, 1977). They were seen over a period of ten days. Seven were women, and there was no correlation with the menstrual cycle. Two were on birth control pills, and two were post-menopausal. Eight of the ten had signs of cerebellar dysfunction, detected by abnormal heel to toe, Romberg, and finger to nose tests, and possibly indicating early cerebral edema. The point to be noted from this study is that it may be associated with severe acute mountain sickness.

EVALUATION AND TREATMENT OF PERIPHERAL EDEMA IN THE FIELD

When one area of edema is observed, other areas should be looked for as well. If hand edema is present, one should check for tight rucksack straps, constrictive clothing around shoulders, arms or wrists and evaluate sun and cold exposure. Rings should be removed while it is still easy to do so.

Facial edema should be taken more seriously, although it *may* be completely harmless. Swelling due to sunburn is obvious. In itself, facial edema is not an indication for descent. If the eyes are swelling shut, however, it can be quite serious, since it will affect vision. Treatment with descent or diuretics is then indicated. A diuresis (marked increase in urine) usually starts while descending, but may be delayed one to two days. If edema is a significant problem, Lasix can be administered orally in a single dose of 40 mg. and this is usually sufficient. A repeat dose of 40 or 80 mg. (one or two tablets) can be given six to twelve hours later if necessary.

Leg edema can be treated with elevation of the feet to a point above the heart. Have the person lying down with feet on a rock, for example, whenever resting. Ace wraps can be applied to help squeeze the excess fluid back into the body core. If boots become tight (and therefore possibly putting one at risk of frostbite) or impossible to wear, Lasix is indicated in the same dose as above, in addition to the other measures mentioned.

All persons with peripheral edema must be checked for pulmonary and cerebral edema and if these signs are not present, it is safe to continue on.

If high altitude pulmonary edema (H.A.P.E.) or cerebral edema (C.E.) is present, immediate descent is mandatory.

If mild acute mountain sickenss is present (no H.A.P.E. or C.E.), then severity of the symptoms and of the peripheral edema determines the treatment, if any is necessary.

Persons should not be advised to stop the ascent or to descend solely on the basis of uncomplicated peripheral edema.

Classification of Acute Mountain Sickness and Treatment

4

THERE is no grading system or standard nomenclature commonly accepted or agreed upon by those studying the subject, and this creates obvious problems. I find it useful to try to divide acute mountain sickness into three categories--mild, moderate and severe. Others may not. What *is* important is to know how to differentiate minor and harmless mountain sickness from serious and life-threatening forms.

MILD ACUTE MOUNTAIN SICKNESS

By mild acute mountain sickness is meant the presence of a few symptoms which are more of a nuisance than a threatening illness. For example, a mild headache, some insomnia and anorexia, and shortness of breath when exercising. I also call this group of symptoms (which is by far the most common presentation) "feeling the altitude." Most persons with mild acute mountain sickness are able to continue their ascent, perhaps taking medications to reduce symptoms. Instead of taking a number of medications for the various symptoms, as discussed earlier, it may be safer and more effective to take only one--Diamox. (See Diamox, Chapter 8.) By aiding acclimatization (probably by causing an increase in breathing), it helps to relieve the cause of the problem rather than just treat the symptoms. The symptoms, however, usually will clear spontaneously in 24 to 48 hours. Mild acute mountain sickness should be taken as a warning that one needs more time to acclimatize, and it is best to stop and spend an extra day or night acclimatizing if possible. This will prevent progression to moderate acute mountain sickness. People less tolerant of the symptoms usually need to descend only 200 to 300 meters for relief, and then can often re-ascend the next day.

MODERATE ACUTE MOUNTAIN SICKNESS

Moderate acute mountain sickness means progression of symptoms to the point where one is quite uncomfortable. The headache may be severe, and only partially relieved by aspirin or aspirin with codeine, if relieved at all. In addition, there is often lassitude, weakness, loss of appetite with perhaps nausea, and difficulty with coordination. There may be some breathlessness at rest. At this stage, there is usually a reduced urine output. This is the stage at which acute mountain sickness must be recognized and dealt with correctly to avoid a real tragedy. Practically all cases of severe mountain sickness are preceded by the moderate form as just described. Stoic individuals may fail to mention their symptoms to companions or even try to conceal or deny them. They are often the ones who must be carried down later or who die on the mountain.

Persons with moderate mountain sickness must stop ascending. Although one may be strong enough to continue, judgment and coordination are often impaired, and rugged terrain becomes hazardous to the sick person as well as his companions. If there is no improvement after a few hours (or overnight if one has camped) then descent is necessary. Actually, the earlier the descent, the more rapid the recovery. If ataxia is present, a longer descent may be necessary for recovery. Otherwise, 300 to 600 meters (or 1,000 to 2,000 feet) is usually adequate. If descent is done early in the course of moderate acute mountain sickness, re-ascent after recovery in two or three days is often possible. If, for some reason, descent is impractical or impossible, oxygen, if available, should be administered. Lasix may be given in a single dose of 80 mg.

39

orally or 40 mg. by injection into a muscle or a vein. Fluids should be given by mouth simultaneously to avoid severe dehydration from the Lasix. If ataxia is present, dexamethasone can be given. (See Cerebral Edema.)

SEVERE ACUTE MOUNTAIN SICKNESS

This is essentially the presence of fulminant pulmonary edema and/or cerebral edema. This category obviously overlaps with moderate acute mountain sickness. It is only a matter of gradation of symptoms from moderate acute mountain sickness to high altitude pulmonary edema or cerebral edema, although some experts feel that H.A.P.E. is a separate entity from mountain sickness. The debate is irrelevant for our present purposes. Let us first discuss cerebral edema.

5   Cerebral Edema

CEREBRAL edema develops generally over
the course of a few days. Thus, it is quite unlikely to
happen on Mount Rainier, for example, where altitude exposure is usually limted to two days and
maximum sleeping altitude is 3,000 to 3,400 meters.
But it is not uncommon in the Everest region, where
altitude exposure is at least seven days and maximal
sleeping elevation varies from 5,000 to 5,700 meters,
and much higher and longer for climbers.

The symptoms are essentially the same as moderate acute mountain sickness but more severe. Headache, vomiting, ataxia, lassitude and reduced urine
output dominate the clinical picture. In as many as
two-thirds of the cases, there is also evidence of fluid
in the chest and some pulmonary symptoms such as

41

breathlessness or cough. The time course in the Everest region is usually 24 to 48 hours of mild acute mountain sickness followed by 24 to 48 hours of moderate acute mountain sickness, and then as ataxia and lassitude become more severe, coma (deep unconsciousness) may ensue in another 12 to 24 hours, if there is not intervention. Rarely, there will be unconsciousness with only 24 hours of preliminary symptoms. Changes in consciousness may be dramatic. A victim is sometimes completely disoriented and confused—he cannot even recognize his companions, and may have some amnesia. (Hypothermia can also present with these symptoms.) There may be hallucinations. (One of our recent patients was convinced he saw a red helicopter outside our door, and he could not understand why we didn't let him get in it, so that he could be evacuated.) He may lie quietly in a tent, not getting up for meals, not speaking, not even going out to pass urine or have a bowel movement (severe lassitude). Often the cerebral edema victim is left alone on the assumption that he is just exhausted and irritable, or perhaps depressed. All one has to do to make the diagnosis is to have him try the heel to toe test or Romberg test (see Ataxia). Even severe lassitude without ataxia is enough for mandatory descent.

We have never seen convulsions (seizures) with cerebral edema, although it has been reported. Different types of paralysis have been observed at our clinic which we felt were secondary to cerebral edema—two VIth nerve paralyses (causing lack of full eyeball movement) and assorted hemipareses or hemiplegias (weakness or paralysis on one side of the body).

A physician equipped with an opthalmoscope can diagnose cerebral edema by observing swelling of the optic nerve in the back of the eye, a condition called papilledema. Physicians should do such examinations on anyone at altitude with a severe headache or other neurological symptoms. The diagnosis can then be made before it progresses further. The absence of papilledema in someone with cerebral manifestations of mountain sickness, however, does not exclude the diagnosis.

TREATMENT

Descent is the only definitive therapy (as of 1980). It should be done as rapidly as possible and as far down as possible. As soon as the condition is recognized mobilization should be started. Taking someone down in the middle of the night instead of waiting until morning may save a life or prevent long term brain damage. Delaying descent to wait for a rescue team, a helicopter, or a doctor is gross "malpractice," assuming descent is possible.

Oxygen should be administered at four to six liters per minute if available and can be given in transit to a lower elevation. We recommend dexamethasone in the hope that it will reduce brain swelling, although no studies have been done on its use in altitude cerebral edema. Dosage is 10 mg. IV intially, followed by 6 mg. IV every six hours if possible. If evacuation is impossible, Lasix can be administered in a dose of 20 or 40 mg. IV, the frequency depending on urine output, blood pressure, and pulse. Severe dehydration, as evidenced by a drop in blood pressure and an increase in pulse, must be avoided. A number of recent studies have shown that the brain can tolerate (survive) low blood oxygen levels, as long as blood *flow* is adequate. It seems to be the reduction in blood flow, due either to low blood pressure or severe brain swelling that causes irreversible damage. Also, it is probably cardiovascular collapse that is the direct cause of death in these cases, and reducing the blood volume by using too much Lasix will only hasten the process.

Osmotic diuretics such as Mannitol suck fluid out of a swollen brain, but are impractical for field use and will not be discussed.

High Altitude
6   Pulmonary Edema

HIGH altitude pulmonary edema is the most dangerous form of acute mountain sickness because its onset may be insidious or quite acute. Some experts report it can progress to life-threatening seriousness in only a matter of hours after it is first noted. This is true because it isn't noticed early enough. Early signs include marked breathlessness on exertion, breathlessness at rest, and decreased exercise capacity. An increased respiratory rate will usually be noted if it is looked for, and often an increased heart rate (pulse). Again, comparison with well people at altitude is useful. It is not uncommon to have respirations of 26 per minute or greater (after a ten-minute rest). Sometimes, however, respiratory rate at rest remains normal until high altitude pulmonary edema is more advanced. The earliest signs may be decreased exercise tolerance, and then a cough. The cough is usually dry until late in the course of the illness; that is, there is no production of sputum. It will be present at rest as well as during exercise.

It is unusual to see high altitude pulmonary edema without other signs of acute mountain sickness, especially headache, lassitude, and reduced urine output, although "pure" H.A.P.E. does occur. Peripheral edema may also be present. Late in the course of H.A.P.E. ataxia develops. Cerebral edema and H.A.P.E. commonly are seen together in the severely ill persons. More than once in our area someone with high altitude pulmonary edema was treated with oxygen only, and not descent, and over the next eight to twelve hours developed cerebral edema as well. Cerebral edema can progress to near death and the lungs sometimes still remain clear. The point to remember is that the distinction between one and the other is not really important, for their significance is the same—death may be only hours away, and immediate action is indicated. There is evidence that the basic problem of acute mountain sickness is abnormal fluid shifts into the brain and the lungs, and although pulmonary *or* cerebral signs may dominate the clinical picture, there is probably involvement of both.

Listening to the chest with a stethoscope is the easiest way to detect early high altitude pulmonary edema. Fluid accumulation results in "rales," a sound resembling the one made by rubbing a lock of hair between the fingers next to one's ear. Professional mountain guides and rescue units should receive training in using the stethoscope. In one study we did of 200 trekkers passing through Pheriche, a full 48 (or 23 percent) had rales present. Although some may have had rales from other causes, it indicated to us that a large number of people at high altitude have excess fluid in their lungs. However, it was not always associated with high altitude pulmonary edema or acute mountain sickness and thus we do not recommend people descend merely on the basis of a few rales and without any symptoms. Such people, however, must be observed closely while they continue ascending. It seems that a large number of visitors to high altitude may have a very mild degree of pulmonary edema, and are in a dynamic state of balance, so to speak, between fluid accumulation in the lungs and removal of that fluid back into the blood vessels. When the balance is upset, for reasons that we still do not understand, fluid accumulation progresses and the result is high altitude pulmonary edema. This theory still remains to be proven.

In advanced cases, there is so much fluid in the lungs that a gurgling sound can be heard without a stethoscope. There is usually copious pinkish or rusty-colored sputum at this point as well. Cyanosis (bluish or blue-grey coloration of the lips and fingernails) develops as H.A.P.E. progresses and blood oxygen becomes dangerously low. A patient's fingernail color should always be compared with your own, and preferably in daylight, outside the tent. (Cyanosis may be detected in cerebral edema also.)

The differentiation of high altitude pulmonary edema from chest infection can be very difficult. In fact, both can be present. It seems that a chest infection (pneumonia or bronchitis) predisposes to development of H.A.P.E. The mechanism is unknown, but probaby involves the increased severity of hypoxia (low tissue oxygen). With a chest infection, there is usually green or greenish-yellow sputum. Fever is common in infection *and* H.A.P.E. Wheezing is heard with both bronchitis and H.A.P.E. Rales are heard in both pneumonia and H.A.P.E. High altitude pulmonary edema is quite rare below 3,000 meters (10,000 feet). The subject with H.A.P.E. appears more desperately ill over the course of hours if continuing to ascend and develops other symptoms such as ataxia. Pneumonia and bronchitis change less quickly. Since both infection and high altitude pulmonary edema may be present, descent is indicated if there is any question of the correct diagnosis. High altitude pulmonary edema will characteristically improve rapidly with a descent of 300 to 500 meters or so, while a chest infection will not. The rule is: when in doubt, go down!

TREATMENT

It is a condition much better prevented than treated. There are three rules for treatment: 1) descent, 2) descent, 3) descent! If detected early enough, a small loss of altitude makes a great improvement. The more severe the high altitude pulmonary edema, the further one may have to descend for improvement. In our experience of more than 100 cases, only two did not recover with a descent of 1,000 meters or less. Oxygen should be administered if available, at a high flow rate (4–6 L/min. if there is enough) *while descending*. We do not use Lasix for H.A.P.E. unless descent must be delayed. In such a case, we give 40 or 80 mg. IV. It can be given orally as well. The use of Lasix in H.A.P.E. is disputed, and there are no studies on its effectiveness in H.A.P.E. Digitalis is not indicated, since heart function has been shown to be normal. Morphine sulfate in small doses of 5 to 10 mg. IV or IM can be given to a severely ill patient who for some reason cannot be immediately evacuated. Steroids have no proven value. The Japanese use acetazolamide (Diamox), 500 mg. IV or IM every eight hours in the treatment of high altitude pulmonary edema. There are no studies available on its effectiveness.

It should be noted that studies from Peru and Leadville, Colorado have shown high altitude pulmonary edema to be more common in well-acclimatized high altitude dwellers who go to lower elevations for periods of a few days to a few weeks, and then return to their home altitudes abruptly. (Interestingly, we do not see this in Nepal.) Dr. Hultgren has shown that in such persons, rest and oxygen, and in mild cases, rest alone, is sufficient treatment. However, we feel that these cases are not quite the same as visitors to altitude, for whom we recommend more aggressive therapy, i.e. descent. Since oxygen is rarely available, and quite precious when it is, and since it may or may *not* be truly effective, whereas descent is *always* effective, there is little question in our minds as to the value of descent. While in the past we routinely called for helicopters for H.A.P.E. victims (a minimum wait of 24 hours) we no longer do so, for in eight to twelve hours we can descend someone by yak or back 1,000 meters (3,000 feet), giving oxygen in transit if necessary. (This method also saves the victim the considerable cost of a helicopter ride!)

Antibiotics are indicated when 1) there may be a chest infection present as well, and 2) evacuation is delayed and the possibility exists of a superimposed infection developing. Penicillin, ampicillin, tetracycline, or erythromycin may be administered in doses of 250 mg. four times a day.

Positive pressure breathing devices have been advocated. The concept has proven useful in pulmonary edema from other causes at sea level, although the exact mechanism of its effect is unknown. Such devices are rarely available, however, and their use might delay descent. This method has not yet been field-tested, and is not recommended.

A person who has had high altitude pulmonary edema once is probably more likely than others to have it again, especially if the same altitude is reached at the same rate of ascent. By going much slower, however, it may be prevented from recurring. Diamox may also be useful for prevention. (See section on Diamox.) We have had two cases of persons with H.A.P.E. who went to lower altitude to recover and came back up to the initial altitude without problems. When they proceeded higher, however, H.A.P.E. struck again.

Fluid Balance
7 At High Altitude

THE decrease in the relative humidity of the cold, dry air of the mountain environment, combined with rigorous exercise, results in marked insensible fluid losses. The respiratory passages moisturize all air inhaled, but do not reclaim the moisture in the air exhaled. One to two liters of water (without salt) can be lost this way each day at moderate altitudes. It is much worse at extreme altitudes (greater than 6,000 meters or 20,000 feet). Sweating also takes place more freely in the dry air (with loss of salt). Adequate fluid replacement may be difficult because of lack of water above the snow line, arid terrain, nausea, etc. Sweating can be fairly well controlled by adjusting layers of clothing and one's pace. Panting or excessive breathing from too fast a pace should be avoided. The thirst reflex may be blunted at altitude, so that one becomes progressively more dehydrated unless a *conscious* effort is made to drink a large amount of fluid.

One way to gauge dehydration is by monitoring the urine output. Scant amounts of dark yellow urine indicate dehydration. The lighter the color and the more frequent the urination, the better the state of hydration.

People on initial exposure to altitude, if they are going to acclimatize well, seem to experience a diuresis. Thus they pass more urine and it is a light color. This is the result of fluid shifts taking place in the body, the reasons for which we do not yet understand. Those who are most likely to acclimatize poorly, it seems, do not have this spontaneous diuresis. They may pass urine just as they do at lower altitudes or at sea level.

As acute mountain sickness develops in these persons, they have an actual anti-diuresis. The urine becomes scant and they may show signs of excess fluid retention, such as peripheral edema, high altitude pulmonary edema or cerebral edema. Thus urine output becomes an important indicator of one's adaptation or maladaptation to altitude.

The Himalayan Rescue Association has been recommending that all trekkers and climbers drink whatever amount is necessary to maintain a clear and copious urine (at least 1½ liters per day). We have found this to be effective in aiding acclimatization, although the exact mechanism is unclear. It may be that dehydration aggravates the tendency toward acute mountain sickness. Indeed, some of the symptoms of acute mountain sickness may actually be due to dehydration, which can cause nausea, dizziness, and weakness. Important for us to know is that persons with reduced urine output have it not on the basis of dehydration from poor fluid intake, but on the basis of a true antidiuresis from (or causing) acute mountain sickness. Thus by recommending everyone to be well hydrated, the symptom of reduced urine output becomes more significant, and more obvious as well.

Clinical signs of dehydration to look for include dry throat and tongue, dry skin, and postural changes in blood pressure or pulse. To detect these changes, have the person lie down and rest for a few minutes. Take the pulse by palpating an artery (the radial artery in the wrist is the easiest) and counting the number of pulsations in 30 seconds. Multiply times two to give the pulse for a full minute. Then have the person sit up with legs dangling or stand up. Wait 30 seconds, and take the pulse again. If the pulse in the upright position is twenty per cent greater (usually fifteen beats or more difference), the person is considerably dehydrated. Giving Lasix in such a situation could be disastrous, by making a litter case of someone who is still strong enough to walk. The problem is that a victim of acute mountain sickness can have low blood volume, as demonstrated by postural changes, and *still* have edema of the brain and lungs. In such cases, we administer fluids orally or by IV and give Lasix as well. Do not give Lasix to a dehydrated person who is incapable of taking in fluids.

Salt tablets are generally unnecessary, at least in our area. Excessive sweating, however, can lead to salt and water losses resulting in volume depletion. This is best prevented by controlling perspiration and drinking adequate fluids. One must not be lazy and neglect to stop and remove a layer of clothing if necessary to diminish sweating. Pace can be set to reduce overall heat production. In the presence of *excessive* sweating and dehydration, in addition to fluids (one or two liters) salt tablets may be administered, one tablet for each 8 ounces of water. However, if people need more salt, they will usually add more to their food. We had an American oil engineer living in Indonesia who was accustomed to using salt tablets whenever exercising in the tropics. He was also using them in the Himalayas, eight a day, although his sweating was minimal. His companions were also living in Indonesia, but left their salt tablets at home. They spent ten days above 4,000 meters (14,000 feet), going over passes of 5,500 meters

(18,000 feet). Everyone was feeling stronger and better acclimatized with each day, except the engineer, who slowly deteriorated to the point where his friends brought him down to be checked. He had mild pulmonary edema! The excessive salt had undoubtedly caused excessive fluid retention. He discontinued the salt tablets and went back up to higher altitude without further problems. We recommend people avoid extra salt prior to a large gain in altitude. Most foods, especially processed ones, have more than enough salt.

Prevention of Acute Mountain Sickness

8

ACUTE mountain sickness is much better prevented than treated. There is now good evidence that simple preventive measures can be effective. In the Mount Everest region, on Mount Kenya, and on Mount McKinley the incidence of deaths and evacuations for severe AMS has been markedly reduced in the past few years. In 1975, in those who flew to 2,900 meters (8,840 feet) and then started trekking to the Everest Base Camp (5,300 meters/16,155 feet) the incidence of acute mountain sickness was 69 percent. Two years later, after a preventive education campaign by the Himalayan Rescue Association, the incidence had declined to 43 percent. The number of trekker deaths from acute mountain sickness was down from three or four per year to none in 1977, 1978 and 1979. These same preventive recommendations are presented here, with slight modifications.

GRADED ASCENT

In those individuals susceptible to acute mountain sickness, the faster the rate of ascent, the more likely they are to develop symptoms. Prior to altitude exposure, one presently has no way of knowing or predicting performance at altitude. Those who do well at altitude will most likely do well again, given the same rate of ascent. Those with repeated exposures seem to do better each time, in fact. However, throwing all caution to the wind, and steaming up to altitude will often make one realize his "AMS threshold." Then again, differences in hydration, exertion, diet, etc., may alter one's susceptibility to acute mountain sickness on any given exposure. For newcomers to altitude we recommend:

- Do not fly or drive to high altitude. Start below 3,000 meters and walk up.

- If taken passively to altitude, do not exert yourself or move higher for the first 24 hours.

- Once above 3,000 meters, limit your net gain in altitude (your sleep altitude) to 300 meters per day (1,000 feet).

■ Carry high and sleep low. It is best to go a little higher than the sleeping altitude, and then descend, instead of sleeping at the maximum altitude reached that day. Camp in valleys, for example, instead of high ridges between valleys, while you are acclimatizing.

■ Take an "acclimatization" night for every 1,000 meters gain in elevation, starting at 3,000 meters or so. (Thus every three days while still ascending.) This means sleeping at the same altitude for two consecutive nights. The day can be spent relaxing or hiking up a ridge, bouldering, or whatever, depending on how you are feeling. People with symptoms of acute mountain sickness should rest.

Even those with considerable altitude experience are advised to follow these recommendations to derive maximum benefit of acclimatization. It may mean the difference between a marginally enjoyable struggle and a comfortable, thoroughly enjoyable (and safe) trip. Why suffer?

When going for a summit, a pass, a view from the ridge top, etc., much longer ascents can be made in a day, secure in the knowledge that one will descend the same day and not actually sleep more than 300 meters to 500 meters higher than the previous night. It is the *sleeping* altitude that is critical. So, for example, Mount Rainier can be climbed from a sleeping altitude of 3,000 meters to the summit (4,400 meters) and back down in a long day. If one had to sleep on top, risk of acute mountain sickness would be high without an intermediate camp. Once fairly well acclimatized (after one to two weeks at altitude, depending on the individual), ascents of 1,000 to 1,500 meters can be done easily in a day, except at extreme altitude (over 6,000 meters).

PREVENTION OF DEHYDRATION

As noted earlier, we recommend all persons to drink enough fluids to maintain a clear and copious urine. Reduced urine output in the face of adequate intake is a hallmark of poor acclimatization. The mechanism in play here is poorly understood, and we admit the evidence for our recommendation is anecdotal rather than scientifically established. (See Fluid Balance at High Altitude.) Nevertheless, we find this recommendation quite useful.

AVOIDANCE OF OVEREXERTION

We recommend care be taken not to overexert at altitude. Packs should be lighter than one's usual lower altitude load. The rest-step should be used when going up steep hills. Panting or excessive breathlessness, or a racing pulse (greater than 135 to 145) are indications to slow down or to stop and rest.

A lengthy recovery time for pulse and breathing to return to normal may indicate early pulmonary edema.

HIGH CARBOHYDRATE DIET

We recommend a diet high in carbohydrates. There are a number of studies in both humans and animals that show higher blood oxygen levels are achieved during the first few days of altitude exposure with a diet of 70 to 80 percent carbohydrates. Such a diet was also shown to reduce symptoms of acute mountain sickness. Also, many expeditions and studies have reported that fatty foods become unappetizing at altitudes above 5,000 meters. However, with prolonged stay at altitude, it is probably the reduced appetite with subsequent low energy intake that causes overall physical deterioration, and thus the total number of calories becomes more important than the proportion of carbohydrates and fats. For this reason, palatability of the food becomes a crucial factor.

MEDICATIONS

There are no medications which we recommend routinely for prevention of acute mountain sickness. Indeed, we feel strongly that medication for this purpose may be harmful, both because of side effects, and giving one a false sense of security. Each nationality of trekkers or climbers passing through Pheriche has its favorite chemical prophylaxis. None have been subjected to controlled studies except two diuretics, furosemide (Lasix) and acetazolamide (Diamox). The Indian Army obtained excellent results with furosemide as prevention for acute mountain sickness but other researchers have found it not to be effective, and in fact, detrimental. Lasix is a very potent diuretic which acts by increasing excretion of salt by the kidney. As salt is excreted, water follows. It should not be used haphazardly, and preferably only by experienced laymen, or physicians. We feel that it should not be used prophylactically.

Acetazolamide (Diamox), it is now generally agreed, does reduce the incidence and severity of acute mountain sickness (and we now also use it to treat mild AMS). This has been determined statistically on large numbers of people. For a given individual, however, the medication in no way should be thought of as a *guarantee* of freedom from mountain sickness. Serious mountain sickness has been reported, although rarely, in persons taking Diamox.

Until recently, it was thought that for effective prevention Diamox must be taken one or two days prior to ascent. We now know that it works quite quickly, and does not have to be started until the day of the ascent, or even after reaching high altitude. Diamox can be taken for the first few days at altitude and then discontinued, or continued until the highest altitude is reached. If symptoms of acute mountain sickness occur when the medication is stopped (as has been reported on two occasions on Mount McKinley), it should be immediately started again. Dosage is 250 mg. (one tablet) twice a day. Side effects most noted are numbness and tingling in fingers, toes, or face (thought to be related to direct action on peripheral nerves) and an increase in urine output, which may be a considerable inconvenience in extreme conditions (we recommend wide-mouth water bottles or tin cans as urine containers in the tent). Some persons have reported a sluggishness or mild depression while using Diamox.

Its exact mechanism of benefit is unknown. It is a mild diuretic. It does make the blood a bit more acidic, thus allowing one to hyperventilate more (and raise the lung and blood oxygen content) without experiencing the symptoms of hyperventilation. It also decreases the cerebrospinal fluid pressure by slowing its formation, and has recently been shown to be a respiratory stimulant during sleep at high altitude (Sutton et al., 1979). This latter action may be the most important. This remains to be proven.

As one can see, it is a powerful drug, and should not be regarded lightly. Therefore, it is not recommended routinely. There are, however, two indications for its use for prevention. One is in the situation of a rescuer or rescue group to be transported abruptly to altitude. In such a situation, use 250 mg.

every eight hours. If there is a chance of remaining at altitude overnight, adequate oxygen supplies should be transported as well. The second indication is for a person who routinely experiences acute mountain sickness, even with gradual ascent and following the recommended preventive measures. Such a person is more susceptible to acute mountain sickness than others because of individual physiological characteristics. For these people, Diamox may be an alternative to giving up the mountains in favor of the beaches.

Aluminum hydroxide sodium carbonate (Rolaids) has been suggested as a prophylaxis for acute mountain sickness (Penberthy, 1977). It is incorporated into a four–point prevention program designed for Mount Rainier climbers which includes: 1) adequate hydration, 2) high carbohydrate intake while climbing, 3) Rolaids to maintain the urine pH at 5.5 to 6.5 (slightly acid), and 4) regulating climbing pace to keep the heart rate (pulse) below two-thirds of maximum. It is the opinion of this writer that such a program on Mount Rainier is of obvious value in preventing acute mountain sickness, even *without* the use of the Rolaids. There has not, as of this writing, been a controlled study on the use of Rolaids and although there are no noted harmful side effects in the dosages recommended, we do not recommend its use as mountain sickness prophylaxis.

Other drugs such as cocaine, methoxamate (Lucidril), and others which are mentioned from time to time in the lay or medical literature are of unproven value and possibly harmful. It seems unlikely that marijuana in usual dosages has any effect on acute mountain sickness or acclimatization, although it has not been studied. Excessive alcohol (drunkenness) is thought to be harmful. High doses cause dehydration and also may contribute to cerebral edema. It has been shown in dogs to increase pulmonary artery pressure at simulated altitude, which could worsen hypoxia and conceivably contribute to pulmonary edema. Local Sherpa wisdom dictates never to get drunk the first night at altitude.

Although there are no studies on the effect of cigarette smoking in acute mountain sickness, it is known that the small amount of carbon monoxide inhaled while smoking can interfere with the oxygen transport system. Studies at Pheriche have shown no difference in incidence of acute mountain sickness between smokers and nonsmokers, but the number of smokers studied has been too small to draw firm conclusions.

High Altitude
Retinal Hemorrhage
9   (HARH)

R ETINAL hemorrhages are areas on the retina where bleeding has occurred, producing a dark red discoloration of varying size. They are generally closer to the arteries than the veins, and fortunately are only rarely in the macula, the main center of vision.

Dr. Charles Houston was the first to report high altitude retinal hemorrhages, in 1968. He noticed them in subjects taking part in his High Altitude Physiology Study on Mount Logan, at an elevation of 5,200 meters. Since then, there have been numerous reports in the medical and climbing literature, and a number of investigations. Their exact cause, however, is still a mystery. There is recent evidence that HARH may be related to lowering of the blood's oxygen content during sleep.

At sleeping altitudes above 5,200 meters they are quite common, reported in 30 to 60 percent of subjects studied. At lower altitudes, such as Pheriche (4,240 meters), they are less common but more likely to be associated with acute mountain sickness. High altitude retinal hemorrhages will clear completely in one week to a few weeks, depending on their size and depth. They rarely affect vision subjectively, although minor defects may be demonstrated with careful testing. *Symptomless retinal hemorrhages are not an indication for descent* and cannot be detected except by opthalmoscopy, which requires a special instrument and training. Persistent visual changes at altitude may be due to retinal hemorrhages or retinal edema, or to problems behind the eyes, that is, in the brain. Symptoms such as double vision or noticeable blind spots are indications for immediate descent, and usually start to clear rapidly at lower elevation. Blurriness of vision is relatively common, may be due to edema of the retina, and clears on descent.

In our area, high altitude retinal hemorrhage is more common in women. In one Everest expedition, it was noticed to be more common in newcomers to the sport while uncommon in climbers with repeated exposures. Much more research needs to be done to determine susceptibility, pathophysiology, and true significance of HARH. It is indeed a sobering thought that the same kind of bleeding we see in the retina may be happening in the brain as well.

References

Carson, R. and Evans, W., "Symptomotology, Pathophysiology, and Treatment of Acute Mountain
Sickness," *Federation Proceedings* 28:1085–1091, 1969.

Hackett, P. and Rennie, D., "Rales, Peripheral
Edema, Retinal Hemorrhage and Acute Mountain
Sickness," *American Journal of Medicine* 67:214–218,
1979.

Hackett, P. and Rennie, D., "Acute Mountain Sickness," *Lancet* 1:491, 1977.

Hackett, P. and Rennie, D., "The Incidence, Impor-
tance, and Prophylaxis of Acute Mountain Sickness," *Lancet* 2:1149–1155, 1976.

King, A. and Robinson, S., "Vascular Headache of Acute Mountain Sickness," *Aerospace Medicine* 43:849, 1972.

Singh, et al., "Acute Mountain Sickness," *New England Journal of Medicine* 280:175, 1969.

Sutton, J. et al., "Effect of Acetazolamide on Hypoxia During Sleep at High Altitude," *New England Journal of Medicine* 301 (24):1329-1331, 1979.

Suggested Reading

Heath, Donald and Williams, David, *Man At High Altitude*, Churchill Livingstone, London and New York, 1977.

Wilkerson, James, *Medicine for Mountaineering*, The Mountaineers, Seattle, 1975.

Houston, C., "Altitude Illness—1976 Version," *American Alpine Journal*, 50:407–415, 1976.

Houston, C., "Altitude Illness—Recent Advances in Knowledge," *American Alpine Journal*, 53:153-159, 1979.

Houston, C., "High Altitude Sickness," *Backpacker Magazine* No. 27, June/July, 1978.

Rennie, D., "See Nuptse and Die," *Lancet*, November 27, 1976. (A brief but excellent summary of current knowledge in the field with an extensive bibliography, for doctors and physiologists.)

APPENDIX: MEDICATIONS FOR USE IN THE TREATMENT OF AMS

DRUG	INDICATIONS	DOSAGE (ADULTS ONLY)	SIDE EFFECTS/PRECAUTIONS C: COMMON O: OCCASIONAL
Oxygen	severe headache severe insomnia at extreme altitude cyanosis pulmonary or cerebral edema	Six liters/minute initially. After improvement, can reduce to 2 to 3 L./min. Give enough to keep patient's color good. Do not delay descent in favor of oxygen.	No adverse effects. Must have tight-fitting mask. Oxygen reservoir bag helps.
Acetazolamide (Diamox)	for prevention (see text)	250 mg. (1 tablet) twice a day starting the day of exposure, and continuing for 3-5 days at altitude or until highest altitude reached.	C—tingling in hands, feet, face; increased urination O—makes beer taste strange; fatigue
	for treatment of AMS	250 mg. 2 or 3 times a day.	
Acetaminophen (Tylenol)	headache	500 to 650 mg. every 3 to 4 hours as necessary	Side effects uncommon with correct dosage
Aspirin	headache, fever	500 to 650 mg. every 3 to 4 hours as necessary	O—stomach irritation
Codeine	severe headache	15 to 30 mg. every 3 to 4 hours as necessary; best to take in combination with	O—stomach irritation C—nausea; constipation; drowsiness O—restlessness

Drug	Indication	Dosage	Notes
		If required continuously for more than 24 hours, descent is indicated.	
Dexamethasone (Decadron)	cerebral edema	IV or IM: 10 mg. initially, followed by 6 mg. every 6 hours if possible (IV or IM). Continue until patient improved. Do not delay descent. Gradually reduce dosage over 2 days or more before discontinuing.	Many side effects in long-term use. Few if used less than 3 to 4 days.
Diazepam or Flurazepam (Valium or Dalmane)	for insomnia	Valium: 5 to 10 mg. at bedtime. Dalmane: 15 to 30 mg. at bedtime.	O—"hangover" feeling in morning; in overdose produces ataxia. DO NOT MIX WITH ALCOHOL
Furosemide (Lasix)	moderate AMS pulmonary edema (sometimes) peripheral edema (see text)	40 to 80 mg. orally, IM or IV (see text).	C—weakness; dehydration O—low blood pressure Best used by physician only except for peripheral edema.
Morphine sulfate	pulmonary edema in extremis (see text)	15 mg. IV for an average sized adult	C—drowsiness, euphoria O—respiratory depression; low blood pressure, confusion. Best used by physician only.
Promethazine (Phenergan)	nausea & vomiting useful for nighttime cough	25 mg. orally or intramuscularly	C—dryness of mouth. O—dizziness; blurred vision.

Notes

Notes